Musical Therapy

At Home, Church, and in the Community

Dion Lucas and Deborah McNeal

TEACH Services, Inc.
P U B L I S H I N G
www.TEACHServices.com • (800) 367-1844

World rights reserved. This book or any portion thereof may not be copied or reproduced in any form or manner whatever, except as provided by law, without the written permission of the publisher, except by a reviewer who may quote brief passages in a review.

The author assumes full responsibility for the accuracy of all facts and quotations as cited in this book. The opinions expressed in this book are the author's personal views and interpretations, and do not necessarily reflect those of the publisher.

This book is provided with the understanding that the publisher is not engaged in giving spiritual, legal, medical, or other professional advice. If authoritative advice is needed, the reader should seek the counsel of a competent professional.

Copyright © 2019 Dion Lucas and Deborah McNeal

Copyright © 2019 TEACH Services, Inc.

ISBN-13: 978-1-4796-1022-8 (Paperback)

ISBN-13: 978-1-4796-1023-5 (ePub)

Bible texts labeled (ESV) are taken from The Holy Bible, English Standard Version. ESV® Text Edition: 2016. Copyright © 2001 by Crossway Bibles, a publishing ministry of Good News Publishers.

Bible texts labeled (NIV) are taken from The Holy Bible, New International Version®, NIV® Copyright ©1973, 1978, 1984, 2011 by Biblica, Inc.® Used by permission. All rights reserved worldwide.

Bible texts labeled (NKJV) are taken from the New King James Version®. Copyright © 1982 by Thomas Nelson. Used by permission. All rights reserved.

Bible texts labeled (KJV) are taken from the King James Version of the Bible. Public domain.

Bible texts labeled (MSG) are taken from The Message, Copyright © 1993, 1994, 1995, 1996, 2000, 2001, 2002 by Eugene H. Peterson.

Table of Contents

Ministry 5

Unison 7

Sowing 9

Inspirational 11

Charismatic 13

Attentive 15

Listening 17

Thinking 19

Harmony 21

Encouragement 23

Rhythm 25

Acapella 27

Pitch 29

Yielding 31

Ministry

The **M** in "**M**USICAL THERAPY" represents ministry. Studies have shown musical therapy to be a key component in a person's overall wellness because it's a universal language that speaks to all nationalities, ages, and genders. Listening to a variety of music creates balance, especially for musicians when creating new materials for audiences. Therefore, musical therapy is a ministry that can impact our homes, churches, and communities.

Music can soothe the mind for relaxation while driving and help students/athletes perform well in school and in athletic competitions. It can increase memory while studying and improve speech communications. Also, daily chores can be done with a pep in our steps to the sounds of music as our bodies move to a rhythm. Individuals can feel a burst of energy throughout their day; and musical therapy can have calming effects to prepare for the night in order to have a peaceful sleep. Even health advisors recommend musical therapy to children and adults of all ages to improve their intellect and moods because "a joyful heart is good medicine, but a crushed spirit dries up the bones" (Proverbs 17:22, ESV).

In churches, the singers and musicians set the atmosphere for pastors or ministers to share divine messages with their church congregations. School pep bands can encourage student-athletes to persevere and give their best performances throughout the entire athletic event. Inspirational selections at community gatherings can create an essence of hope when tragedy hits our homes and families. Overall, music can provide comfort to all mankind, no matter what season of life we are facing. Rest assured that seasons do change, and we should be open to new musical artists who will provide uplifting songs across our world.

Unison

The **U** in "**MUSICAL THERAPY**" represents unison. "If a house is divided against itself, that house cannot stand" (Mark 3:25, NIV). We are often told that "united we stand and divided we fall" to encourage all of us to collaborate and unite with each other to maintain peace in our homes and communities.

Members in a music department inside or outside of the church must come together in unison and support each other in ministry. When singers and musicians are bonded together, a sweet expression is felt in church that ushers in the presence of the Lord. "For He Himself is our peace, who has made the two groups one and has destroyed the barrier, the dividing wall of hostility" (Ephesians 2:14, NIV).

Sowing

The **S** in "**MUSICAL THERAPY**" represents sowing. No one performs well at any task without practice. Remember this: "whoever sows sparingly will also reap sparingly, and whoever sows bountifully will also reap bountifully" (2 Corinthians 9:6, NKJV).

Parents encourage their children to do and study their school work. Coaches rally their athletes to master their craft. Likewise, musical directors emphasize the importance of practice to their singers and musicians because it is key to being successful. Great accomplishments at home, in the church, and out in the community only come by sowing a seed of greatness and having a good work ethic to sustain a bountiful harvest.

Inspiration

The **I** in **"MUSICAL THERAPY"** represents inspiration. "All scripture is given by inspiration of God, and is profitable for doctrine, for reproof, for correction, for instruction in righteousness: that the man of God may be perfect, thoroughly furnished unto all good works" (2 Timothy 3: 16–17, KJV).

God orchestrates our lives from day to day through His Word because He is our true conductor. The Lord declares, "For I know the plans I have for you … Plans to prosper you and not to harm you, plans to give you hope and a future" (Jeremiah 29:11, NIV). Therefore, "Whatever your hand finds to do, do it with all your might" (Ecclesiastes 9:10, NIV).

Serving in a music ministry is a wonderful privilege. Singers and musicians must continue to inspire congregations across the world, to let them know that we serve an awesome God and He deserves our best praise. Never quench the gift that God has given you in the music ministry. Always give your all to God!

Charismatic

The C in "**MUSICAL THERAPY**" represents charismatic. Charismatic means exercising a compelling attraction which inspires commitment in others. Therefore, the music ministry has the power of winning the devotion of large numbers of people by the anointing of the Holy Spirit through praise and worship.

"Now to each one the manifestation of the Spirit is given for the common good" (1 Corinthians 12:7, NIV). God has given each person spiritual gifts and talents to share the gospel among people in our homes, churches, and communities. "For we are His workmanship, created in Christ Jesus unto good works, which God hath before ordained that we should walk in them" (Ephesians 2:10, KJV).

Attentive

The first **A** in **"MUSICAL THERAPY"** represents attentive. "Shew me thy ways, O Lord; teach me thy paths. Lead me in thy truth, and teach me: for thou art the God of my salvation; on thee do I wait all the day" (Psalm 25:4–5, KJV).

When God speaks to you in a song, you must be attentive to the message rather than the rhythm and beat. Inspirational songs can provide words of comfort for those who may be grieving over a loss of a loved one. Also, the message in gospel songs can heal a broken heart. That is why it is crucial to be attentive to God's words in spiritual songs because a beat is meaningless without His direction.

The music ministry attends to both our vertical and horizontal divine expressions. Vertically, singers and musicians give praises to our God above and are guided by the Holy Spirit on how to offer songs of comfort. Horizontally, we sing together in the congregation which links us as brothers and sisters. Always remember our attention must never be on self but on God. He can handle all our problems and lead us on paths of righteousness for Christ's sake.

Listening

The **L** in "**MUSICAL THERAPY**" represents listening. "Wise men and women are always learning, always listening for fresh insights" (Proverbs 18:15, MSG). People make good decisions if they listen to the advice of parents, instructors, and coaches.

Also, staying in tune to the direction of the Holy Spirit is pivotal in a music ministry. Even though plans are made for services, song selections may change due to messages from a minister or pastor to the congregation. Worship is not static—not something that can be rehearsed—but it is an organic experience that uplifts us all in our lives.

Thinking

The **T** in "**MUSICAL THERAPY**" represents thinking. "Trust in the Lord with all thine heart; and lean not unto thine own understanding. In all thy ways acknowledge him, and he shall direct thy paths" (Proverbs 3:5–6, KJV).

Giving God our best praise requires singers and musicians to give 100% effort at rehearsals and worship services. The music ministry does require a lot of thought into scheduling rehearsals and selecting songs for worship services. Directors may rehearse songs to sound just like the original audio recordings. However, things may change on a moment's notice depending on how selections impact the congregation. Remember to be flexible to the movement of the Holy Spirit and trust in God to adjust plans to work out for good.

Harmony

The **H** in "**MUSICAL THERAPY**" represents harmony. "Make every effort to keep the unity of the spirit through the bond of peace" (Ephesians 4:3, NIV). Voices harmonizing together are a pleasing combination of elements that completes an ensemble. Having unity in any organization is important, and it is a key component in a music ministry. Remember this: "Live in harmony with one another. Do not be proud, but be willing to associate with people of low position. Do not be conceited" (Romans 12:16, NIV).

Encouragement

The **E** in "**MUSICAL THERAPY**" represents encouragement. Musical therapy is first introduced to children by their parents or guardians. Many professional singers and musicians were taught their crafts in the church. The choir directors would teach singers how to hold a microphone and project their voices, and band directors would perfect musical selections as if every service was a live-recording worship extravaganza.

However, there are times in a music ministry where burnout can occur and in those times, we must encourage each other with God's Word and keep up the good fight of faith. Remember this: "But they that wait upon the Lord shall renew their strength; they shall mount up with wings as eagles; they shall run, and not be weary; and they shall walk, and not faint" (Isaiah 40:31, KJV).

Rhythm

The **R** in "**MUSICAL THERAPY**" represents rhythm. Musical rhythms can help project the melodies of a song or rap and engage listeners. For example, Christian rap is being used now in music ministries to reach a contemporary audience. "Let everything that has breath praise the Lord" (Psalm 150:6, KJV). Although people can rock to the beat of a Christian rap, it's important that the message being delivered is positive and uplifting. Having children rap about God is much better than having them speak words of violence and hatred in our communities.

Acapella

The second **A** in "**MUSICAL THERAPY**" represents acapella. Singing songs or delivering sermons do not have to be accompanied by music. People often times get distracted by the rhythm of the music and miss the meaning behind the message. Therefore, we must not lose focus on the power of God's holy words. We ought to "praise him for his acts of power; praise him for his surpassing greatness" (Psalm 150:2, NIV). The lyrics of a hymn or gospel song are to be the main focus so that hearers can journey upward on the Christian's pathway.

Pitch

The **P** in **"MUSICAL THERAPY"** represents pitch. All singers and musicians must maintain pitch to avoid any distractions when ministering to congregations in a corporate atmosphere. Psalm 150:1 tells us to "Praise the Lord. Praise God in his sanctuary" (NIV). However, private worship settings give freedom for all singers and musicians to express themselves in whatever key their hearts desire. May God continue to set the tone for our days and bless our futures as we minister through song.

Yielding

The **Y** in "**MUSICAL THERAPY**" represents yielding. God will guide us in all areas of our lives as we submit to His counsel. The Holy Spirit will take our music ministries to higher levels that will encourage people in our homes, churches, and communities to give their lives to Christ. "Therefore, if anyone is in Christ, the new creation has come: The old has gone, the new is here" (2 Corinthians 5:17, NIV).

TEACH Services, Inc.
PUBLISHING

We invite you to view the complete
selection of titles we publish at:
www.TEACHServices.com

We encourage you to write us
with your thoughts about this,
or any other book we publish at:
info@TEACHServices.com

TEACH Services' titles may be purchased in
bulk quantities for educational, fund-raising,
business, or promotional use.
bulksales@TEACHServices.com

Finally, if you are interested in seeing
your own book in print, please contact us at:
publishing@TEACHServices.com

We are happy to review your manuscript at no charge.

www.ingramcontent.com/pod-product-compliance
Lightning Source LLC
Chambersburg PA
CBHW061119170426
43200CB00023B/2996